EXTREME

sports

mountain biking

BARRON'S

contents

Mountain biking has come a long way since it started in the 1970s. Then, some cyclists in California had fun riding bikes known as "clunkers."

These bikes became the mountain bikes we know today. Now, mountain biking is an Olympic sport.

The great thing about this sport is that it has something for everyone. Try racing at high speeds or the thrill of doing stunts and tricks. Or just go out there and ride and see new places.

This book will show you some of the amazing things you can do on a bike.

cross- country racing

Cross-country racing is the most popular competition on mountain bikes. Most races are a number of laps around a course that is usually between three and seven miles (6 to 12km) long.

Racing at the top level is tough and riders have to be very fit. But anyone can compete, no matter how fit they are. There are races for every level of rider from beginner upward. It's a great challenge.

downhill

racing

Downhill is the most exciting type of racing. It's a race against the clock. Most races have one rider at a time going down the run. There are also courses where two riders race against each other.

World Cup downhill racing is really extreme. The riders go at great speeds and keep pedaling even down the very steep hills. They usually wear special body armor, pads, and a full-face helmet to protect themselves. It's a tough sport and you need to be prepared to take some knocks.

riding for fun

This is what most people do on mountain bikes – just going out and riding. You might follow a route or go exploring. It might be for a couple of hours, a whole day, or even a tour lasting weeks or months.

On short rides all you need is a basic tool kit if you know where you're going. Always take a good map on new routes. On longer rides you may need to take some food and extra clothes with you.

For touring, you'll need bike bags to carry all your gear. Or take a backpack – it's up to you.

tricks

and stunts

This is the extreme side of mountain biking.
Many riders have tried a trick or two.
For some riders it's what they do most of the time.

You should start by learning the basic moves.
Expert stunt riders take these basic moves and turn
them into the extreme tricks you see here.

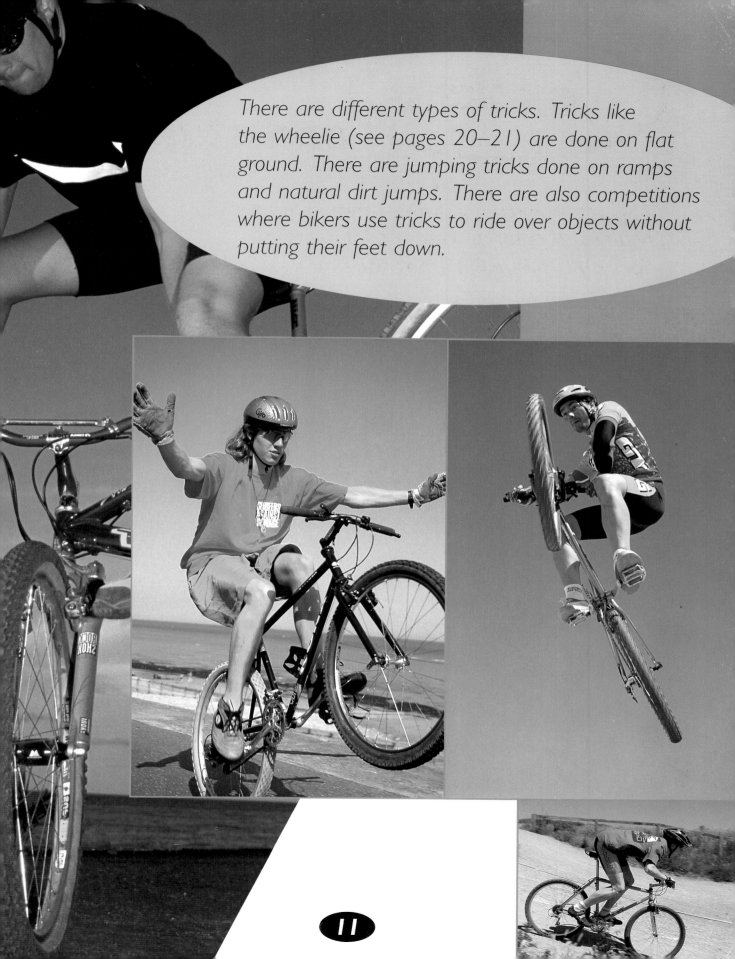

There are different types of tricks. Tricks like the wheelie (see pages 20–21) are done on flat ground. There are jumping tricks done on ramps and natural dirt jumps. There are also competitions where bikers use tricks to ride over objects without putting their feet down.

mountain bikes

When it comes to buying a bike, you get what you pay for. Always try to buy a well-known make.

Find a good bike shop. They will help you make the right choice. They should let you test ride any bike before you buy it. You can read bike magazines to find out which are the best buys.

brake lever

gear grip

front brake

front gears

pedal

back gears

bars

Cross-country racing

Touring

Downhill racing

saddle

Tricks and stunts

back brake

There are different types of bike for the different types of riding (shown above).

clothing and equipment

You can go biking in any type of clothing. But you will be more comfortable if you wear clothes that are specially made for cyclists.

Shorts

A good pair of cycling shorts will help you feel more comfortable in the saddle.

Shoes

Cycling shoes have soles that are quite stiff. Some riders prefer a sneaker with a softer sole—particularly for tricks.

Waterproofs and thermals

These are great for keeping you warm and dry when the weather gets bad.

Helmet

A good, well-fitting helmet is very important for safety. Never go biking without wearing one.

Glasses

Glasses protect your eyes from sun, dust, insects, and branches.

Jerseys

Cycling jerseys are usually long at the back to cover you when you lean forward.

Gloves or mitts

These will keep your hands comfortable and protect them if you fall off.

Repairs

You'll need a pump and a puncture repair kit. A good wrench is useful for tightening loose bolts. If you need to do more serious work on your bike, get a good book on repairs.

getting started

Before trying anything difficult you need to know the basics of riding.

There are two main things to learn –

1 **How to steer your bike and use the gears and brakes.**

Start gently. Practice riding around a flat area at a slow speed. Get a feel for using the brakes. Try using different gears to see what they do. Do figure eights and slow, small circles. This will help you control your bike.

Now go a bit faster. Try to stop without locking the wheels or skidding. This way you can practice your brake control. Don't "grab" at your front brake as this can throw you over the handlebars.

2 How to move your body to help your bike turn and go up and down hills.

When riding up steep slopes, shift your body forward. This will stop the front wheel from lifting up. Don't shift too far or your back wheel will not be able to grip.

When going downhill, shift your body backward. Don't shift too far or you won't be able to steer your bike.

Lean your body to the side when you take corners at speed.

riding over an object

It's useful to know how to ride over objects on a trail. You can also do it for fun as a stunt. Find something small to practice on before moving on to bigger things. Riding up onto a curb is an ideal place to start.

1 *Ride toward the object. Make sure you have enough speed to get you over. Push down on the handlebars, ready to pull up. Get one of your pedals up, ready to push down.*

2 *Just before your front wheel hits the object, pull up the bars. At the same time push down on the pedal.*

3 Lift your front wheel higher than the object.

4 Let your front wheel come down on top of the object. Then move your body forward.

5 Now get your back wheel up. Either let the wheel bump onto or over the object, or help it up by lifting up on the pedals with your legs.

6 Let your speed carry you safely over.

the wheelie

This is a simple trick that everyone loves to learn. It's fun to do and looks good. Learning it will help you go on to do more difficult tricks.

1 Choose a medium or easy gear. Push down on the bars, ready to pull up. Get one of your pedals up, ready to push down. Be ready to use the brakes.

2 Push down on the pedal. At the same time, pull up on the bars. The front wheel should lift off the ground. Throw your body back enough to keep the wheel from going back down again.

3 Keep pedaling to keep the bike moving. Use the back brake to stop it from tipping over backward.

4 To stop the bike from falling over sideways, turn the bars and move your body to balance. Keep going as long as you can.

drop-offs

A drop-off is used when you want to ride down a step in the trail or go down steep slopes for fun.

You can take it slowly, leaning back off the saddle. Or you can really go for it and do a wheelie over the edge.

the bunny hop

This is a useful way of jumping over an object on a trail when you're going quite fast. It also looks good. There are competitions to see who can jump the highest.

1 Ride toward the object quite fast. You should be standing on the pedals. Crouch down slightly with your knees and elbows bent.

2 Just in front of the object, spring your body up. At the same time, pull the bike up underneath you. This should lift the bike off the ground.

3 Your speed will carry you over. Get ready to land.

4 Bending your knees and elbows will make the landing smoother.

3

4

getting air

Flying through the air is a great feeling if you do it right. Good riders can get way up into the air. They make amazing shapes with their bodies and bikes.

Try a simple jump to begin with. Keep your elbows and knees bent before you make the jump. As you go up into the jump, straighten your body. Keep the bike straight.

You don't need to pull the bike up unless you want to go really high. Remember to bend your knees and elbows when you land.

Once you're happy with this you can really turn on the style . . .

drifts  and skids

Drifts are fast turns used when the ground is loose or slippery. They're often used in races.

Skids are usually done by accident when you brake too hard. But they can be fun to do on purpose.

Skids and drifts will damage the trails, though. Save them for places like gravel fire roads and BMX tracks.

The idea is to stay in control. Don't use your front brake. This will usually throw you over the bars. You will probably need to lean forward a little. This will allow the back wheel to slide. Then grab the back brake, lock up the wheel, and tear up the ground!

extreme

mountain biking

Extreme bikers are always pushing themselves to do more and more amazing stunts. You wouldn't normally expect to see some of them done on a mountain bike – like jumping into water or off the roof of a house, even up walls and trees.

If someone has thought of it, someone else has probably done it or is planning to do it. The only thing that limits you is your imagination.

extra stuff

Disclaimer

Text and photos: Steve Behr
Thanks to Jill Behr

Series editor: Matthew Parselle
Designer: Andy Stagg

First Edition for the United States and Canada published exclusively by Barron's Educational Series, Inc., 1998.

First published in the United Kingdom 1997 by Franklin Watts, London
Copyright 1997 Franklin Watts

Address all inquiries to:
Barron's Educational Series, Inc.
250 Wireless Boulevard
Hauppauge, NY 11788
http://www.barronseduc.com

Library of Congess Catalog Card No. 98-071482

ISBN 0-7641-0796-8

Printed in Great Britain

Useful Contacts

Adventure Cycling Association
Tel: (800) 721-8719

International Mountain Bicycling Association (IMBA)
Tel: (303) 545-9011

Index